This book celebrates the arrival of

my cat's

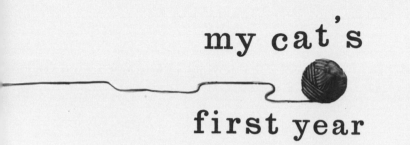

first year

a journal

POP PRESS

in case of loss, please return to:

_____

_____

_____

_____

contents

life is better with cats

Welcome to your journal for your new cat's first year with you. Whether you have just welcomed a kitten into your home or adopted an older cat, this is the place where you can record all the magical memories you'll share together over the next year. This book will also provide you with information on how to prepare for their arrival, as well as handy tips and fun DIY instructions on how to make your own cat treats and toys.

Every cat is different and has a unique personality and set of characteristics. It can sometimes take a while to learn about their likes and dislikes or how to tell what mood they're in based on their behaviour. You can use the notes sections as a place to document your cat's progress and development over the next year, as well as writing down things you learn about them along the way, or even any funny or sweet moments you want to remember.

This is a very exciting and rewarding time, for both you and your new family member. We hope that this journal will be helpful, but that it will also be something you can look back through to remember the special moments you will experience together over the next year.

stick your cat's
photo here

about my cat

born on

....

weighed

....

colour

....

markings

....

he/she had .... siblings

we first heard about our cat from

....

....

we chose this breed because

....

....

....

....

we first visited our new cat on

....

our cat's name

....

this was chosen because

....

....

....

our cat's mum is called

her story

our cat's dad is called

....

his story

....

....

NOTES

16

cat-proofing our home

To get ready for our cat's arrival, we:

- Put away treasured possessions they might chew, swallow or knock over.

- Removed poisonous plants – such as lilies.

- Put dangerous chemicals away out of reach.

- Tidied away electrical wires, small children's toys, elastic bands, hairbands, string or wool – if they swallow these they could get twisted up inside them.

For our cat's arrival we bought:

essential stuff

- Litter tray
- Cat litter
- Water bowl
- Food bowl
- Bed
- Collar
- ID tags
- Grooming brush
- Stain remover!
- Toys
- Scratching post
- Food
- Treats

did you know?
A group of cats is
called a clowder.

home is where
the cat is

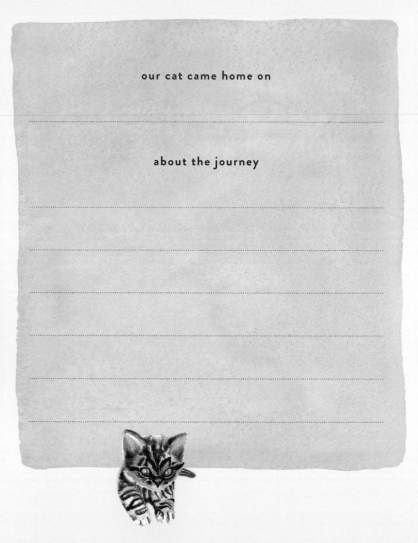

our cat came home on

about the journey

Photos of our cat's first day with us!

tips for
the first days
at home

- Try to collect your cat early in the morning so you have the rest of the day to settle them in.

- Let them out of the carrier in one room so they can get to know the space – let them find the litter tray, food and water bowls.

- Slowly introduce other people and animals.

- Make sure children know not to be rough – no pulling of ears, whiskers or tail.

- If using a cat carrier as a bed, make it comfy, and keep the door open so that they can go in and out. Perhaps leave a few pieces of food in there to show it is a happy place. This is also a good idea for getting them used to using it later when travelling.

the first things our cat did in our home

....

....

....

....

....

....

things that went really well

....

....

....

things we need to work on

....

....

....

did you know?

Cats sleep on average between 16 and 20 hours
per day, and kittens need plenty of opportunities to
rest and for peace and quiet in the first few days.
So make sure they have a comfy bed to go to.

sleepy kitty

their bed is in

....

we made it cosy by

....

....

where the cat preferred to sleep!

....

....

....

'Cats leave
paw prints
on your
heart'

paws for Pawsterity

Here are our cat's paw prints

Date ....

kitty food diary

There are lots of things to consider when it comes to feeding routines as each cat is different.

- Unless your cat has a medical condition, deciding whether to give your cat wet or dry food is completely up to you and you can always alternate between the two. Try your cat with both to see what they prefer.

- Cats like to be fed little and often, but generally two meals a day is fine for most cats. See what works for you. Think about investing in an automatic cat feeder if you want to feed them while you're out.

- Try to feed your cat in the same place each day, in a quiet area where they can relax (far away from their litter tray).

- Choose a surface that can be easily cleaned, or use a feeding mat.

Most cats prefer to have a routine when it comes to food.
Use the table below to help you keep a record of what
works best so that you can establish a routine
as soon as possible.

DAY	TIMES OF DAY	WHAT KIND OF FOOD	TREATS
sunday			
monday			
tuesday			
wednesday			
thursday			
friday			
saturday			

things that worked well

....

....

....

things we will try in the future

....

....

....

our cat's eating spot

....

favourite meal

....

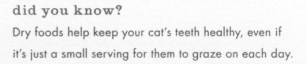

did you know?

Dry foods help keep your cat's teeth healthy, even if
it's just a small serving for them to graze on each day.

first time our cat ate a new food

....

....

our cat's favourite treat is

....

....

....

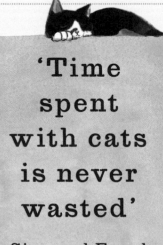

'Time
spent
with cats
is never
wasted'

Sigmund Freud

tips for
getting to know
each other

Playing with your cat and stroking them are great ways to socialise them and develop a really special bond.

Use long, slow strokes over their entire body with your hand, from their face to their tail (base to tip).

Kittens need to get used to being touched on their ears; older cats may have to have their ears cleaned and examined, so use a light touch inside each ear (don't use anything in the ear canal itself), and pull back the outer ear to see right inside.

Gently open your cat's mouth and look at their teeth; put your finger in between the lip and the teeth and run your finger over the surface of their teeth.

NOTES

'You had me at meow'

tips for
playtime
training

**Teaching your cat to play nicely from an early age
will make playtime more fun and less painful!**

 Don't use your fingers as toys – if you have a kitten, their teeth and claws might be tiny, but they will get bigger, longer and sharper.

 If your cat gets over-excited and bites you, stop what you're doing and stay as still as possible. If you're not moving, it's not as much fun; they will soon learn that biting or scratching means playtime stops.

 Use cat toys: fishing-rod toys are great, as are throwing toys – both keep your cat's claws and teeth clear of your fingers.

favourite cat toys

handsome
kitty

we first groomed our cat on

....

we used

....

....

how they reacted!

....

....

....

The finished result!

NOTES

welcome home!

the first visitors were

....

....

....

they came on

....

they brought

....

....

....

training your cat to come when you call

If your cat will be going outside, training them to come to you when you call is a good idea.

step 1

Decide on a word that you want to use to call your cat – not their name, and not a word you use for anything else.

step 2

Start the training when they are relaxed (but not sleepy).

top tip:

When cats first go out it's very exciting and new so they may need extra treats to tempt them back!

step 4

Repeat this a few times every day, and they should start to associate the word with the treat.

step 5

After a while, move further away or even go into the next room to call them.

step 3

Sit on the floor close to them and say the call word, holding out a treat.

step 6

When your cat is old enough to go outside, practise calling them!

tips for
out and about

Cats are happy indoors or out, you can decide, depending on their personality, health issues, history, your own circumstances and the local area. There are several options:

Indoor only
Your cat can be happy and fulfilled indoors with plenty of environmental enrichment, toys and playtime.

Restricted access outdoors
You could construct a catio, or outside pen, at your home, so they get the best of both worlds. They are protected from certain dangers, but get to enjoy fresh air, sunshine and wildlife (without the wildlife being at risk from their hunting instincts).

Supervised access outdoors
Another good compromise: your cat can go outside into your garden with you. You can even take them out on a leash!

Unsupervised access outdoors during the day

If you get your cat into a routine of being fed at a certain time in the evening, or train them to come when you call, you could keep them in at night.

Unsupervised and unlimited access outdoors

If you have a cat flap and leave it unlocked 24/7, your cat will be able to come and go as they please. Just beware other local cats taking it as an invitation to come in; to avoid this you might want to get a microchip flap.

garden safety checklist

If your cat will be going outside into the garden, there are a few possible hazards to be aware of:

- Cover up any ponds or water features.

- Check the plants and flowers you have growing to make sure none are toxic to cats.

- Make sure there are no chemicals or potentially toxic substances lying around.

- Tidy up any broken glass, jagged edges, or sharp objects.

training your
cat to walk
on a leash

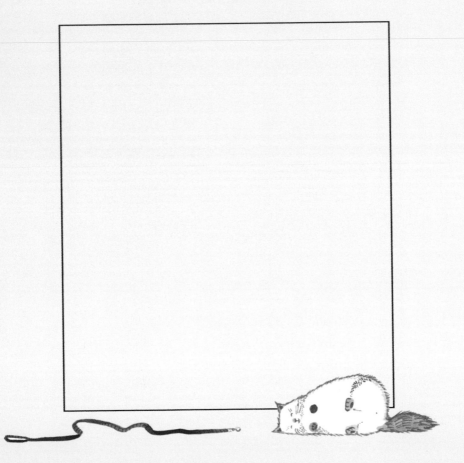

If you want your cat to experience the great outdoors without being at risk of traffic, predators or possible poisons, leash training is a great solution.

Getting the right leash and harness
You'll need a leash and harness made for cats that fits around their body.

Getting used to the leash and harness
Leave the leash and harness around so your cat can get used to the sight and scent of it.

Putting the harness on
Distract your cat with treats when it's first on – it will be strange to them at first.

Attaching the leash
Once your cat is happy wearing the harness you can attach the leash. After a few days of putting it on them, start picking up the end of the leash and letting your cat walk you!

Ready to explore
When your cat is happy on the leash you can start taking them outside into a quiet place, like the garden.

did you know?

A cat's nose is ridged with a
unique pattern, much like a
human's fingerprint.

NOTES

NOTES

exploring the great outdoors

Our cat's first outing

Date ....

tails from our cat's first outings

they were nervous of

they were excited by

Here is our cat chilled out at

....

they were calm and relaxed during

NOTES

NOTES

kitty language

Now our cat has lived with us for a few weeks, we can tell
what they're thinking by watching their body language.
This is how we can tell they are:

happy:

over-excited:

scared:

hungry:

just being
greedy!:

bored:

not feeling well:

tired:

meow!

SOUND THEY MAKE		WHEN THEY MAKE IT
	>	
	>	
	>	
	>	
	>	
	>	

Your cat might make a lot of noise, but what do you think
each different sound means?

They may purr when you stroke them under their chin,
chirrup when they're pleased to see you, or meow when
they want you to feed them (again!). Have you worked
them all out yet?

WHAT DOES IT MEAN?

our cat's favourite...

toy

....

spot in the house

....

place in the garden

....

time of day

....

the
disappearing cat

Cats are very skilled at playing hide-and-seek, and there are a number of reasons why they will hide:

 They've found a comfy and secure place to snooze.

 Something has scared them – perhaps you have visitors or there has been some kind of commotion in the home.

 They are not feeling well – this is a natural instinct to hide somewhere safe and protected, as they would in the wild.

If you want to know where they are, create safe hiding places for them that you know about:

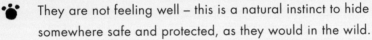 Have lots of cat beds tucked away in peaceful corners (igloo beds are great).

 Put comfy blankets on shelves and furniture.

what are their favourite hiding places?

what places might be dangerous?
(inside the washing machine, for example)

first trip
to the vet

we took our cat to meet the vet on

....

the vet is called

....

they said

....

....

....

....

top tip:
Why not take your cat to meet the vet just as a fun outing, so later visits –
for injections, etc. – won't be scary? Or just get them used to the cat carrier
by leaving it out and open around the home, perhaps with a blanket and a
favourite toy inside?

how to make a DIY cat house

You don't have to buy expensive cat beds, you can make your own DIY cat house.

You'll need:

An old T-shirt

A cardboard box the right size to pull the T-shirt over

A cushion or blanket that fits inside the box.

A stapler

1. With the box upright, cut the 4 top flaps off so it's open at the top.

2. Turn the box on its side so the opening is facing you, and put the cushion or folded up blanket inside.

3. Pull the T-shirt over the box with the neck hole across the opening.

4. Tuck in the T-shirt's arms and staple the T-shirt at the back to secure it to the box.

The finished cat house!

active mind, active kitty!

A healthy cat needs to be physically and mentally fit; playing together with interactive toys helps give their mind as well as all their senses a workout.

Have fun with boxes
Put boxes of different sizes next to each other and watch your cat jump in and out, or cut holes into a box and put toys and treats inside so your cat has to work to get them out.

Stimulate hunting instincts
Hide their favourite toys in various places around the home for your cat to hunt out. To give them a clue, rub toys with catnip first (or keep them in a sealed plastic bag with catnip).

Make mealtimes a puzzle
Make your cat work for their food and use their hunting instincts. Split meals into smaller portions and place dried food in bowls around the home.

NOTES

'A home
without a
cat is just
a house'

how to
make a DIY
uzzle feeder

Here's my cat using their DIY puzzle feeder

You can buy puzzle feeders – from tiny hollow mice they have to bat with their paw to knock biscuits out of, to large mazes they have to grab and push the food out of – or you can make your own using empty plastic bottles or tubs with holes cut out for biscuits to be knocked out of, or toilet roll tubes cut to different lengths and stuck to a piece of cardboard.

You'll need:

6 empty toilet roll tubes

Craft glue

1. Glue 3 tubes together in a row, and set aside to dry.

2. Glue another 2 tubes together in a row, and set aside to dry.

3. Once dry, layer the row of 3, the row of 2 and the single remaining tube like a pyramid, gluing each row onto the next.

4. Add dried food or biscuits.

playtime

our cat's favourite games

Playing

toys, toys, t✿ys,

You don't have to buy lots of toys, your cat can turn a few normal household objects into amazing fun!

- Screwed-up balls of paper ....

- Shoelaces ....

- Empty toilet roll tubes ....

- Paper bags ....

- Plastic bottles – you could even put treats inside an empty bottle to make a quick DIY puzzle feeder ....

- Socks ....

- Empty boxes ....

our cat's favourite games

how to make DIY cat toys

If you're feeling crafty, making your own toys is a brilliant idea. Here are two easy DIY cat toys you can make:

Sock Snake

One of the easiest DIY cat toys, all it needs is a little sewing skill.

You'll need:

An unwanted sock

Some tissue paper or newspaper

Needle and thread

Catnip (optional)

1. Crumple up the paper and stuff it into the sock (cats love noisy toys!).

2. Sew up the end so it resembles a snake.

3. To make it even more appealing you could mix catnip in with the paper.

Ribbon Cat Wand

You'll need:

A stick or rod

String or twine

Ribbons (cut to lengths of 10–12cm)

1 or 2 small bells (optional)

1. Bunch the lengths of ribbon together (as many as you like) and tie around the top with string to secure them. Tie the other end of the string to the stick.

2. You can add bells to the ribbons if you like, but make sure they're very tightly fastened or they could be a choking hazard if they come off.

My ideas for cat toys ...

Here's my cat playing with their
DIY cat toys!

'One cat
just leads
to another'

Ernest Hemingway

b_ad kitty!

first time our cat scratched or
damaged something they shouldn't

....

it was

....

....

and it belonged to

....

how to make home-made cat treats

While shop-bought treats are great, making your own treats can be fun and more cost-effective! Here are two ideas:

Tuna Treats

You'll need:

A tin of tuna in spring water (drained)

1 egg

180g plain flour

120ml water

A sprinkle of catnip (optional)

1. Preheat your oven to 180°C/350°F/gas mark 4.

2. Blend the tuna with the egg, flour, water and catnip (if using) to make a dough.

3. Break off small pieces and roll into teaspoon-sized balls.

4. Flatten slightly into little biscuits, then bake for 15 minutes.

5. Leave to cool, then store in an airtight container.

Chicken Crumbles

You'll need:

1 chicken breast
(minced)

1 egg

A sprinkle of catnip
(optional)

1. Preheat your oven to
   180°C/350°F/gas mark 4.

2. Combine all the ingredients in a
   mixing bowl.

3. Spread the mixture out on a non-stick
   baking sheet, then bake for 15 minutes.

4. Leave to cool, crumble into little
   pieces, then store in a sealed
   container in the fridge.

My ideas for cat treats ...

My cat's homemade treats!

oh you
paw thing!

first unwanted guests (fleas, etc.)

....

first present brought in to us (dead or alive!)

....

it was

....

about the first time our cat was ill

....

....

....

did you know?
Cats use their whiskers
to detect if they can fit
through a space.

our cat's
first birthday
with us

their presents were

....

....

....

as a treat we

....

....

the cake was made from

....

Birthday fuss!

how to make a cat cake

Chocolate is toxic to cats, so baking a human-style birthday cake is a no-no, but why not try this recipe to celebrate your cat's first birthday? (Even better, there's no baking required!)

You'll need:

Your cat's favourite cat food (in an individual tin or tray)

Some shredded cooked chicken

Some favourite biscuits or cat treats

A cooked prawn

1. Carefully open the tin or tray and empty the cat food onto a dish, trying to keep the shape as much as possible.

2. Add a layer of shredded chicken, followed by a layer of biscuits or a sprinkle of treats.

3. Decorate the 'cake' with the prawn.

My cat's birthday cake –
what a masterpiece!

NOTES

did you know?

Cats can make 100 different vocal sounds. The more you talk to your cat, the more they will talk to you, so make sure to chat to your cat as you go about your day.

our favourite memories so far

*very important pet

vip* information

name

vet and phone number

....

....

date of birth

insurance number

....

....

breeder/rescue and
phone number

insurer and
phone number

....

....

injections due

microchip details

10 9 8 7 6 5 4 3 2 1

Pop Press, an imprint of Ebury Publishing
20 Vauxhall Bridge Road
London SW1V 2SA

Pop Press is part of the Penguin Random
House group of companies whose
addresses can be found at global.
penguinrandomhouse.com

Penguin
Random House
UK

Copyright © Pop Press 2019

Author: Charlotte Cole
Illustrations: Good Wives and Warriors
Design: Emily Voller

First published by Pop Press in 2019

www.penguin.co.uk

A CIP catalogue record for this book is
available from the British Library

ISBN 9781785038624

Printed and bound in China by
Toppan Leefung

MIX
Paper from
responsible sources
FSC® C018179

Penguin Random House is committed to a
sustainable future for our business, our readers
and our planet. This book is made from Forest
Stewardship Council ® certified paper.